Book web

Inspector Grub And The Jelly Bean Robber

Written by Quentin Flynn

Illustrated by Brent Putze

Contents Page

Chapter 1. 4
Jubilee Jelly Beans is robbed!

Chapter 2. 9
An awful smell

Chapter 3. 14
Inspector Grub has an idea

Chapter 4. 20
A jelly bean trap

Chapter 5. 27
A message for the robber

Verse 32

Rigby

Inspector Grub And The Jellybean Robber

With these characters ...

Inspector Grub

Officer Clarke

Officer Murphy

Jessica van Fructose

Mr. Halliwell

Mrs. Hepplewhite

"We need to set

Setting the scene ...

Inspector Grub is on the trail of a jelly bean robber. Why does the robber steal two kinds of jelly beans, but only eat one kind?

It's a mystery with some colorful clues — but will Inspector Grub be able to use them to solve the crime?

a trap!"

Chapter 1.

"Not again!" cried Jessica van Fructose. "Who keeps breaking in to my store and stealing the jelly beans?"

A trail of sticky, green goo oozed across the floor. Two large jelly bean jars lay on their sides, almost empty. Feeling frightened, she locked the door.

Jessica owned Jubilee Jelly Beans. It was the most famous jelly bean shop in the city and on the Internet. Huge jars of colorful jelly beans were displayed in rows along the counter and shelves. Jessica sold every kind of jelly bean — even peanut butter ones.

The most popular jelly beans were the red cherry ones. And, for the third week in a row, most of the red cherry and the green peppermint jelly beans had been stolen!

Suddenly, Jessica heard someone turn the door handle behind her. The door creaked open. Jessica couldn't move. She felt like she was frozen!

"Good morning, Jessica. How was your optometrist's appointment?" Jessica felt relieved. It was only Mr. Halliwell, one of her new store assistants.

"Not again," he said, as he stared at the mess.

"Yes, we've been robbed once more," said Jessica.

Mr. Halliwell rubbed his forehead. "This is frightening! Have you reported it to the police again?" he asked.

“Not yet. I just can’t believe this,” replied Jessica. “I’m sure the door wasn’t open when I arrived just now. Or was it? Oh dear, I can’t remember!”

Just then, Jessica and Mr. Halliwell heard the door creak open behind them. Looking around, they saw the other new store assistant, Mrs. Hepplewhite, standing in the doorway.

"It's only me," she said, happily. Then she looked down. "Oh, no!" she said, looking shocked. "Surely not?"

"I'm afraid so," replied Jessica. "It's the third time this month. Only the red cherry and green peppermint jelly beans were stolen again. This robber has to be stopped. And I know just the person to do it. Call Inspector Grub!"

Chapter 2.

"You're supposed to study the evidence, not step in it!" roared Inspector Grub. Officer Clarke looked embarrassed as he tried to step out of the green goo.

"It's very sticky," he said. Long strings of goo stretched from the floor to his right boot.

“Take your boot off!” ordered Inspector Grub. “I don’t want you tramping evidence through the store!”

Officer Clarke bent down and untied his laces. Then, he slipped his foot out of his boot.

Inspector Grub lay down to study the green goo more closely. His huge moustache almost stuck in the goo. He sniffed. He sniffed again.

“What is that awful smell?” he said, wrinkling his nose and his moustache.

Officer Clarke looked embarrassed. "I *do* change my socks every Monday," he said, with a red face. "They can't smell *that* bad, can they?"

The other policeman, Officer Murphy, sniffed Officer Clarke's socks. He snuffled and sneezed.

"It *is* Friday," he whispered politely.

"Shut up, you two! I can't sniff the evidence with awful-smelling socks and boots around," growled Inspector Grub.

Inspector Grub moved his nose closer to the green goo. He dipped his finger in it and sniffed deeply.

"Peppermint, I think." He stood up. "Miss van Fructose, did you say that most of the peppermint and cherry jelly beans are missing?"

Standing behind the counter, Jessica nodded.

"Well, we've found the peppermint jelly beans," said Inspector Grub. He used his magnifying glass to study the goo on his finger. "Half chewed, and then spat out, I'd say."

“But why spit them out?” asked Jessica, looking puzzled.

“Why half-chew so many of them?” asked Mr. Halliwell, frowning.

“And what happened to the cherry jelly beans?” asked Mrs. Hepplewhite, with her hands open.

Inspector Grub wiped his finger on his handkerchief. “That,” he said, “is what we will find out.”

Chapter 3.

Back at the police station, Officers Clarke and Murphy read from their notes. Inspector Grub listened.

"Miss van Fructose thinks she locked the door the night before," read out Officer Clarke.

"But she can't remember," added Officer Murphy. "She may have left the door unlocked."

"No broken windows or busted doors in the store," reported Officer Clarke.

"Only Miss van Fructose, Mr. Halliwell, and Mrs. Hepplewhite have keys," read Officer Murphy.

"Green and red jelly beans stolen," reported Officer Clarke.

"But the robber spat out the green ones," added Officer Murphy quickly.

"So why steal them?" asked Officer Clarke. Both officers looked up at Inspector Grub, and were shocked by what they saw!

The inspector's eyes were huge and his face had turned red!

"Inspector! What's wrong?" Both officers leaned across the desk.

"I'll do mouth-to-mouth resuscitation," said Officer Clarke.

The inspector let out a loud breath. "Oh, no, you won't!" he roared. "You'll go home and change your socks now! I can't hold my breath any longer!"

The officers rushed towards the door. Officer Clarke's right boot stuck to the carpet with each step. Inspector Grub opened the window and took long, deep breaths.

Inspector Grub looked down at the traffic in the street. The traffic lights turned from green to yellow to red. Breathing normally again, he watched the red traffic lights turn green again.

Suddenly, the inspector had an idea. He made a phone call.

"Hello, Jubilee Jelly Beans! How can I help you?" asked a cheery voice.

"Hello, Miss van Fructose," replied Inspector Grub. "I need some red and green jelly beans right away. We need to set a trap!"

Chapter 4.

On Saturday morning, Inspector Grub sat at his desk with a wide tray and two large jelly bean jars. One jar was full of green peppermint jelly beans. The other jar was full of red cherry jelly beans.

The inspector carefully arranged the green and red jelly beans on the tray.

Officers Clarke and Murphy sat quietly. Both of them were too scared to ask why the inspector was "playing" with jelly beans.

Finally, the inspector stood up from his chair, and looked very pleased.

"Finished!" he smiled. "Now, let's take my trap to Jubilee Jelly Beans."

The two men stared at the jelly beans on the tray. Who would be brave enough to ask Inspector Grub about them?

“Um, well, isn’t it a little . . . a little too obvious?” asked Officer Clarke bravely.

The inspector winked. “Maybe,” he replied. “And maybe not.”

In the middle of the tray of green jelly beans, the inspector had used red jelly beans to spell out five words.

The three policemen sped toward Jubilee Jelly Beans in their police car. Inspector Grub sat in the back seat, squashed between the two jars of jelly beans, carefully holding his tray.

"Watch out for those bumps!" he ordered. The red jelly bean words were becoming blurry.

At Jubilee Jelly Beans, Inspector Grub looked around. "Did you follow my instructions?" he asked Jessica. "Mr. Halliwell and Mrs. Hepplewhite must not work together today."

"Mr. Halliwell will work this morning. Mrs. Hepplewhite will work this afternoon, after he leaves," Jessica replied.

"Good," smiled the inspector. "Now, let's set the trap."

He placed the tray on a shelf under the counter where the customers could not see it.

“Now,” he said, looking very confident, “we will leave and come back at six o’clock.”

Right on time, the policemen returned to Jubilee Jelly Beans. Jessica was waiting for them.

“Nothing has happened, I’m afraid,” she said. “The trap hasn’t worked.”

Officers Clarke and Murphy still hadn't figured out how the trap *could* work — but they didn't dare say anything.

"The trap hasn't worked — yet!" said Inspector Grub. He still looked confident. "Now, let's lock up the shop and go home. We will meet here again at eight o'clock in the morning."

Chapter 5.

The next morning, Officer Clarke looked embarrassed. "Oh, no," he cried.

"Not again!" frowned Inspector Grub.

"I didn't see it," explained Officer Clarke. He tried to pull his boot out of the fresh pile of green goo.

Officer Murphy rushed behind the counter. "There are no red or green jelly beans left on the tray," he reported. "All gone."

Inspector Grub checked the door and the windows. "Nothing broken," he said. "And we know the door was locked properly last night." He spelled out a new word on the tray with the red and green jelly beans.

"What are you doing?" asked Jessica.

"Setting another trap," replied Inspector Grub.

Mr. Halliwell and Mrs. Hepplewhite arrived an hour later. They both stared at the green gooey mess on the floor.

Inspector Grub asked Mr. Halliwell and Mrs. Hepplewhite to come to the counter.

"Can you read this?" he asked politely.

"Yes," smiled Mrs. Hepplewhite.

Mr. Halliwell stared at the jelly beans. "Read what?" he asked.

Inspector Grub asked everyone else to gather around. “Let’s help Mr. Halliwell read this word,” he said. They gathered around and yelled out what was spelled out in red jelly beans.

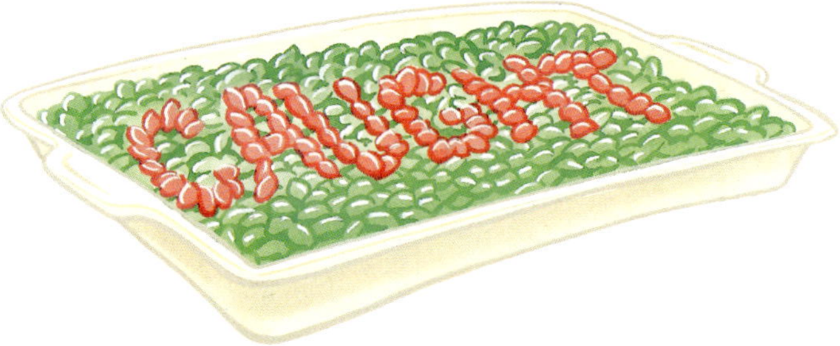

After Mr. Halliwell was taken away, Inspector Grub explained how he had caught the jelly bean robber.

“I got an idea when Mr. Halliwell asked a question about the green jelly beans — ‘Why half-chew so many of them?’ The only answer was that the robber couldn’t tell the difference!”

Everyone looked puzzled.

"Some people can't tell the difference between red and green. The two colors look the same. That's why the trap was obvious to us, but not to Mr. Halliwell. He couldn't see it was a trap. He is *colorblind!*"

Everyone patted Inspector Grub on the back, except Officer Clarke. He was still stuck by the door. He started to untie his laces. Inspector Grub's face turned red again.

"STOP!" he ordered. Officer Clarke looked up. Everyone rushed out the front door, into the fresh air.

"As well as being able to see colors perfectly, we all have a perfect sense of smell," said Inspector Grub. "And there's still one more day until Monday!"

"A warning not seen."

A jelly bean robber
Likes red, not green.
A clever inspector
Writes a warning not seen.

Will the crime be solved?
No one can tell,
And, by the way,
What's that terrible smell?

The trap is set,
But what will they find?
Red and green look the same
When you are colorblind!